Love Poems for Several Men

Love Poems for Several Men

By Leila Pepper

Nazik

Black Moss Press

1997

Published by Black Moss Press, 2450 Byng Road,
Windsor, Ontario, N8W 3E8.

Black Moss Press books are distributed by Firefly Books,
Willowdale, Ontario.

Black Moss Press is grateful for grants from the Ontario Arts Council
and the Department of Canadian Heritage.

We acknowledge the support of the Canada Council for the Arts for
our publishing program.

Black Moss Press would like to thank Paul Vasey
for his invaluable help in editing this manuscript.

ISBN 0-88753-298-5

Contents

I

Landscape With Bleeding Hearts

Coffee House

O to be young again
to have long hair to toss back
to move with the music
small breasts thrust out
throat tight with song
to be part of them all
swaying like lilies in
the breeze of their youth
arrogant   proud-bearing   beautiful!
unaware of how swiftly
it all passes

Reconciling With Death

she waits stiffly
in the chair by the door
when will he come?
she asks
when will he come?
does he know I am here?
this was a poet
a singer
a rider of horses
        my friend
who will take me home?
she asks
when will he come?
let it be swift for us
clean and painless
like lightning
or a sharp knife
but
let it be swift

In Absentia: 1997

rooting through boxes
looking for old letters
I found the pictures

German-occupied Holland: 1945
photographs in black and white
hidden years ago because
I couldn't bear to look at them

dark streets of walking skeletons
children with marble eyes
sunken cheeks and swollen bellies
old men and women degraded
to naked match-stick bones
bodies stacked in carts
like cord-wood
hunger and horror everywhere

we did this to each other
we   God's special creation

tears spill out
hot silly useless tears
tears
for my absent god

After Eye Surgery

Under the patched eye
I see
projected on the retina
pulsing lumps of pink
moving slow tentacles
veined with black
like sea-shrimp
Concentrating on them
for amazing seconds
I am looking inward to
the convoluted brain
As a sky-watcher might view
through his telescope
an uncharted galaxy
I gaze into the depths
of my own mind
Below gauzy filaments
images lurk
faces that change shape
waver   melt into fields
that turn to forests
then become caravans snaking
from shadow to shadow
This imaginary landscape
in the realm of my brain
confounds me
I know each cell
contains a universe   but
in this other universe
what infinitesimal part
is *me*?

Concerning Infinity from a Finite View-Point

Infinity: boundless   endless
says my dictionary
but what preceded infinity?
what will end it?
how can there be Nothing?
even a Bang echoes somewhere
In the Beginning was the Word
what word?   what beginning?
what came before it began?
the mind I have
does not encompass
Nothingness
in the beginning
there was a Garden
but what garden?
coming from where?
never having been able
to add or subtract
I am confused even more
by the mathematical symbol
for Infinity
two inter-locked zeros

Summer Storm

Forgive me
that I am not ready
lightning and thunder
tear the sky around me
hail drums on the roof
rattles my windows
and I try to say
      Lord into Your Hands
for I am shaking with terror
afraid
not so much of dying here
but of what comes after
      that uncertainty
      concerning Heaven
how could it be more beautiful
than the patch of earth
I inhabit   where
this morning before rain
a single butterfly
danced among roses
and the mourning dove
with her coral feet planted
on my garden path
looked at me a long time
before she shook her wings
and arrowed over the fence

The Gospel Singers

In this vast auditorium
this crowded modern temple
you touch us
you eager young men
we sway in unison
a field of blown wheat
heads nod   feet tap
we clap in rhythm to
the songs you sing so lustily
the roof echoes   the walls vibrate
you shout it out triumphantly
your mesmerizing message
that promises us   assures us
we can reach out and touch Him
          Oh yes! Do it now. Reach out
          and touch him. Alleluia!
          Praise the Lord, Amen!

was He there when death came
to the Nursing Home? Could I
have touched Him   felt the wounds?
or was He outside that sad room
far away   too far for me to reach?

is the fault in me
that I sit rigid and resisting
while all around me
persuaded by your eloquence
faith mounts like a great wind
as you beautiful believers
shout the Glory?

Landscape with Bleeding Hearts

Sitting in church
mind wandering
slices of me fall away
revealing
that girl in the convent
silenced
by flickering votive lamps
along carbolic corridors
where nuns glide past
seeming indifferent to
the anguished upturned eyes
of haloed saints   so blue   so gold
so crimson with pierced hearts
nothing is real here except
the remembered smell of incense

the girl who danced
on an upturned boat
under daring stars
one summer night
falls away
falls with the kisses
that broke her heart

the choir is singing
but the words escape me
there is another slicing
to be faced
the sharpest one of all
to remember him lying there
so dead   so very dead

all around me
ruins lie

His Flute

when I cleaned today
I saw it
half-hidden and dusty
lying behind the cranberry glass
my great-aunt left me
then I remembered
heard
the sad sweet notes
coming through midnight mist
as he drifted
alone in the canoe
playing out his sorrow
for a first lost love
heard the flute
crying over the water
crying over the years
as I am now

The Shell Mirror

When he died
I gave away everything
but a worn tweed jacket
hidden in his closet
      and the shell mirror

Get rid of it   throw it away
it will only bring pain
they said of the mirror
lying on my dresser
It is a ring of sea-shells
spiralling periwinkles
glued awkwardly around
a base of shiny foil
when you stare into it
it reflects a crooked image
a tiny distorted face
a kindergarten child
could have made it
but it was carefully crafted
by my husband   at Dayaway
our mutual respite

I remember my fear
the first time he went there
he walked away from me
down the path hand-in-hand
with his driver   then turned
to wave goodbye   and I
felt the same emptiness
I had when our eldest left me
for school years and years ago

Coming home hours later
he told me in a worried whisper
    there were old women
    who couldn't talk!
    Sickies I'd call them
he didn't see himself
ravaged by Alzheimers

Time moves strangely
those old men and women
in short days were his friends
co-workers and buddies
and he was happy because
he was needed   he belonged

in remembering that terrible time
there is pain   one can't forget it
but I remember better how he loved me
and that the mirror
my crooked beautiful mirror
was his last gift of love

Winter Walk

Beautiful in the snow
beside my footprints
bird tracks
printed randomly
undecipherable runes
from an ancient time
in a language I can't read
soon with mine
they will melt away
who knows
what birds these are
waiting for Spring
silent in trees
as darkness falls?
who knows who I am
or where I will be
by Spring?

Another Funeral

The Major
who was eighty-three
died quietly in his sleep
the church is crowded with
wartime comrades and old friends
outside a lone Piper plays
The Flowers of the Forest
the sound of the Lament
comes to us muted   heart-breaking
In the balcony
I gaze fixedly ahead
compressing my throat
so sobs can't escape
here in St. Andrew's
the carved angels stare out
uncaring   unchanged by time
dust lies thick on the wooden dome
high above the organ
I stare fiercely at it
to avoid the flag-draped coffin
with bright claymore
where flowers usually lie
who could climb high enough
even with a tall ladder
to move the ancient dust?
all around me are the faces
of my generation old and wrinkled
looking vaguely familiar like
guests at a masked ball
a sprinkling of Service Men
try to stand erect
but it won't work
they are permanently bent
time has used us all
I watch the wooden angels
today they seem to weep
as I thought they did
when I was young and wondered
why they were so sad
nothing can be held forever
Life   says Japanese poet Mansei
is the white wake of a boat
that rows away in the early dawn

Etching
a Tanka

a single leaf drifts
from the winter-blackened tree
to the frozen ground
far down in the mourning heart
its echo falls endlessly

Questions

Is there an identifiable pattern
something with beginning
and a conclusion like
the well-planned essay
or is it all
aimless   random   purposeless?
at the altar
two elderly women
creaking to their knees
and suddenly   unmistakably
the smell of Paris!
is everything with us always
caught on the wind   glimpsed
from the corner of an eye?
so many pictures
unimportant   irrelevant
is it the frame they hang in
some experience of intense joy
or ancient pain that makes
these images so memorable
returning unexpectedly
to haunt the mind?

Five Hokku

Beneath swift-moving
wheels the red earth slips away. . .
how far my heart lies

with heads together
they sit talking all at once. . .
like crows, the travellers!

His hand rests lightly
on my heart. . . the wild bird knows
what cage awaits it

sharp cry of a loon
shattering the still, cool night. . .
moon-mirror broken

Wind-swept the pine tree
bends unwilling branches down. . .
reluctant servant

Lest We Forget

November 11, 1996
in Ottawa
it is a cold 11.30
the Last Post
has wounded the air
tailored wreaths have been placed
at the foot of the Cenetaph
and the March Past begins
the Armed Forces with the Navy
the Senior Service leading the way
move smartly past the camera
I am remembering our friends
        remembering you
and tears gather in my eyes
I try to hold them back
as I did fifty-five years ago
on that crowded station platform
when we held each other desperately
until you   so handsome
so young in your new uniform
ran to catch the moving train
that would take you away from me
        perhaps forever
I wore a blue-straw hate with field-flowers
and I hoped you would remember my smile

Mysteries

what are they hiding
those low trembling leaves
by the garden wall?
did a bird seek shelter
did a cat creep under
 primed for a sudden pounce
or is it wind   soft wind
tumbling   shifting the leaves
making them shiver
as it passes
and why   watching
do I feel
such exquisite pain
such sense of loss?

The Rose-Bed

Walking in the heat of noon
I see the rose-bed   each petal
shining with drops of water
vivid as a Velasquez painting
The spray falls cool and steady
on the mounded black earth
and its wet plash becomes
all the fountains of Granada
shimmering their spirals
into the bright hot sky
Down vistas of clipped hedges
in a sheltered formal garden
redolent with the scent of oranges
the Infanta walks with her maids
A grotesque and hideous dwarf
grimaces and twirls in her stiff shadow
His monkey eyes dart here and there
trying not to conceal the agony of love
he dare not show to anyone
The fat dueña flutters a silken fan
while beads of perspiration
rim her milk-white forehead
Uncaring Infanta! so safe, so cruel!
What other hearts will you break
before your own is ravished?
The water falls monotonously
heat rises in crystal waves
lulling all my senses   then
grinding truck brakes
shake me into awareness
I stare at a garden sprinkler
showering thirsty city roses

Plane Descending

Down ribbons of time
the plane shudders and drops
as our ears fill   voices
become a murmuring hive
the frantic mind asks
is this the end
instant termination
here and now?   and
for a white-knuckled moment
all answers sway in the balance
Have I a talisman   some charm
to ward off evil   to exempt me
from the imminence of death?
It is too late for prayers
years too late   someone
beside me exhales sharply
as we level off   someone
makes a crude joke
and life comes rushing back
it is laughter one remembers
all the pent-up laughter
of a life-time
bursting forth as
the turbines of the jet
wind down

A.G.D. — 1884-1962

Today I need you
I want you to
come through the door
and put your cool hand
on my head
in spite of fever
I made the necessary calls
paid pressing bills
did the things I should
but still I burn
I can't rest   my bones ache
years ago you were my medicine
Mother   in this old woman
would you see your child?

Cemetery in November

When I returned
the markers were
awash with rain
mats of wet leaves
kindly covered
names and dates
I stood above your grave
sinking in soft mud
feeling no reality
so no tears came
I had shed them
that long year before
as I touched
the flag-draped coffin
shed more a week later
at the gate-house
when they handed me
a jar of grey ashes
last tangible evidence
you had ever lived
it is the wound
of your not-being
that festers and
will not heal

At the Mall

Sitting under a glass roof
in the Picnic Gardens
eating fruit and frozen yogurt
we are Birds of Paradise in
the Botanical House at the Zoo
surreptitiously watching other birds
macaws   toucans   proud peacocks
who strut and turn   fanning
their bright enchanting tails
And because life is eclectic
there are flock of sparrows
and blue-tailed starlings
raucously intruding everywhere
flying from shop to shop
searching boutiques for bargains
This tidal wave bears all forward
to the shore of Fast Foods where
the thin drink Diet Sprite or Coke
the fat lick their lips over
fried chicken or huge slabs of pizza
anchored to paper plates
by ropes of pale cheese
they gorge on French Fries
soggy with stage-red ketchup
or choke on Tex-Mex food
tacos and burritos   firecrackers
in the mouth   everyone is eating
and everything   smells the same
sweet-and-sour   hot-and-fried
On this steamy summer day we have come
to the oasis of air-conditioning hoping
to escape city heat   to cool off
As we gather under captive trees
in this artificial garden   we
compound our discomfort by
bold movements and communal eating
crowded around small tables   those
acres of umbrella-ed duplicates
and although we elbow one another
no one communicates — in isolation
we stuff ourselves as if life
had no other purpose but eating

Healing Service

Hearing you are dead
I spring fiercely to life
drawing your toughness in
recreating myself
in your strong image
this gathering of aged and halt
seeing them so dear
so strangely changed
hurries the process of renewal
I will walk the streets
under turning trees
thanking God I am alive
thankful for the blessing
of being able to see life
moving around me   to see
the bustle of small birds
revelling in a pool of water
from the garden hose
for all the blazing flowers
daring me to endure
thankful even for the blessing of
making my bed with fresh sheets
what glory to be here!
your sudden leave-taking
shaking me   shocking me
has given me a gift

This Thing Time

this thing Time
pushes us
inexorably forward
there are no visible
stops for rest
and somehow
it is always Monday
the longed-for weekend gone
and I am waiting for late mail
when suddenly it becomes Friday
with beds to change
and laundry bulking large
in spite of these revolutions
these subtle turns of the wheel
that moves effortlessly silently
without our will
I stay the same
I stay me
standing solidly somewhere
wondering how it will all end

The Barrier

He builds a fort of piled-up books
and peoples it with soldiers made of lead
I see gay banners floating past, hear
shouts and firm and mail-clad tread
but when he strides the draw-bridge wide
leading brave men who march cross the floor,
though I would enter to be one with him
in his enchanted place, barred is the door.
I am shut out. I cannot follow after.

Awkward he is, and small and thin
with hands and feet grown suddenly too big;
his cowboy clothes are held together
with pins and patches like a scarecrows rig,
yet when he climbs in dizzy spirals
up the gnarled branches of the apple-tree
his is a grace a prince would envy
as he mounts higher and away from me.
I stay below. I cannot follow after.

In a life's span
the boy I cannot follow
and I may not hold the man.

Hypothetical Cases

According to Scientist George Michanowsky:
      If the supernova Alpha Centauri
      were to blow itself apart
      we would all be incinerated, however,
      (an important consideration)
      this is not expected to happen
      IN THE NEAR FUTURE!

 Writer Francis Cornford describes
a soon-to-die-solder as:
      a young Apollo, golden-haired
      magnificently unprepared for
      the long littleness of life.
yet poet Rupert Brooke that
"so great lover," in ironic refutation
was left no time at all
for the trivialities of life.

It is not that we lack
imagination enough to picture
the destruction of our civilization
but this grim *totality*
like the fabled flames of Hell
is incomprehensible, defying belief,
a concept beyond our grasp
No! What really threatens our security
is the loss of little things,
our possessions, trivia, that proclaim
our individuality, our uniqueness

Michanowsky continues:
      a black hole can grow
      and keep growing.
      Somewhere in outer space
      such an object is travelling
      in our direction and will eventually
      DEVOUR US.

God! what a choice!
      to be swallowed up
      in deeper dark than Jonah's
      or to be incinerated?
      Where crawl to hide, how escape
      the smell of burning flesh
      in this new Hell?

Trying to Write

from where I sit
in bright blown leaves
pencil in hand
on the slope of
the October hill
I watch the lake
and listen   I hear
waves cold as metal
scouring the shore
see gulls
sketch the sky
knife-diving where a fish
leaps diamond-wet
yet no words come
I am dust-dry
then   suddenly
the geese
the wild geese honking
as they pass
high over head
a fluttering Vee
following their leader
southward and I
am filled with envy
no soaring flight for me
my way I do not know
all that lies ahead
is silence   with
thick-falling snow

Curtain-Raiser

this early March bare trees
cast shadows on a red-brick wall
bringing excitement   the anticipation
of curtains slowly rising on a
favourite opera   in grey gardens
promises of Spring inch through
the earth to green my passing
today no loud chorus of birds
only here and there greeting the sun
an isolated call   a clear note
that hits the heart hard
being as yet so sweet so rare

So Much For Albert Schweizer

REVERENCE FOR LIFE
a noble concept
one I endorse
I've been a follower
a true disciple for years
or at least until yesterday   I swear
it was two inches long
that centipede in my tub
I screamed   it scrambled
I shuddered   grabbed a weapon
crying out hysterically as
I attacked the ugly creature
with my wet towel and
playing God   squashed it
flushed it down the toilet
so. . .
now where do I stand?

Don Quixote Today

The windmills that you tilt at
are all tomorrows
winter-tree tall and spare
restless feet pawing the ground
you spread out marvellous plans
joyfully sharing a crumpled map
of the new world you will build
the poetry you bring is embryonic
emerging one word at a time
each word a month apart but
pregnant with future meaning
puzzled by our earthly plodding
our wingless density as we try
to follow your soaring flight
you are infinitely patient
without malice or conceit
as innocent   as beatific
as any medieval saint shining
blessings from stained-glass

that you are penniless   homeless
that your wife has left you
destroyed by years of promises
these are unnecessary details
not to be dealt with here
where yesterday doesn't exist
and today is irrelevant.

Invasion

The moon-drenched lake is alien tonight
silver and cold   from the window I stare
at the indifferent stars as they weave
patterns of my childhood and I am sad
thinking of this old cottage when I am gone
I am jealous too knowing that strangers
will hear the dark sound of racing water
as the waves' wild horses   mount the shore
while in the shadowed room behind me there
where flickering candles burn the hours down
some unborn lovers' eyes will hotly hold
across the firm barrier of my oak table
and an intruder who does not care
will take our pictures from the wall

Christmas Week

fog lies over the city
in the staffroom teachers
are discussing clothes
sports jackets   bulky sweaters
they say:
you really pay at Sam's
if you want the good stuff
they say:
Jo's a dude
six watch bracelets
in different colours yet!
one says:
my wife wants a fur coat
now the strident bell
wakens dead corridors
my fingers are ink-stained
my mind as slushy
as the streets outside
where   I wonder
in this fog
does the Manger lie?

Psalm 30: Shall the Dust Give Thanks?

They say that God is dead
the God of the Old Testament
who plucked and uprooted His enemies
devoured them, scattering their bones
to the wind and the wayward sand
Still   we knew where we stood
for a God of Vengeance gave
certain and strong comfort
we were safe when his terrible Hand
destroyed our ancient enemies

That grey-bearded old man
enthroned in the distant sky
protecting His chosen people
faded out with childhood's end
Now in this empty universe
what God does one invoke? To what
Awful Vacuity in time of need
do heart and mind cry out?

View-Point

a found poem

according to Glenn Jones
New Age Messiah
the Info Highway is part of
the neurology of the human mind
extending it in dramatic form
for the first time in history
just as the human body
was extended by the fork-lift
in the Industrial Age
the Cable take-over
is led by Goliaths

in this New Age Order
I am frightened
my sling-shot hangs
limp and useless
from my hand

II

Love Poems for Several Men

Hearing Albeniz's Tango

At my age
I should be ashamed
to remember
my mind should be
on Last Things
repentance   salvation
        and what comes after
but today I burn
I remember your eyes
I remember your mouth
not what you said but
how you looked at me
your arms would be
salvation
I repent nothing.
Yet — how quickly
it all passed!

Postlude

season after season
year after year
hackles up we fought
dancing around each other
arrogant young prize fighters
sparring at the least provocation
using any excuse to argue
eager to wound   to jab at egos
in mounting excitement
we strutted
flexing muscles by
prolonged verbal battles
hot and quarrelsome
proud and conceited
we were well-matched
there was electricity
sparks flew between us
write a poem for me
you challenged
and we both laughed
at such a silly idea

a real war
stopped the war between us

now you are dead
and I can't tell you
I *did* write for you
but what a shock
it was to find
those hidden verses
dearest enemy
turned out to be
love poems

Separation: For H.

Under the blanket of sleep
buried deep I work
all night fragments of things
we used to do spread
in endless disorder
before my heavy eyes
slip from between my hands
loom large a moment
then are gone   it is my task
to sort them out   they are like
the feathers in a fairy tale
always about me and never still
Sometimes I catch them
pinioned a moment   in my heart
the dark glint of your eyes
the turn of your head   and
your smile that pulls
my twisted heartstrings as
the master-hand a puppet's
all night I work
till the harsh clanging
of the rising-bell
startles me up from the depths
and scatters your image
into a thousand pieces

Panic

Although you left an hour ago
your presence clings like smoke
it lingers in the corners of the room
and faintly-heavy curls about
the easy chair in which you sat
I feel it weighing down upon my face
and soft upon my hands and lips
but heavy on my throat   trembling
I raise myself and throw the window wide
to banish you   then turn triumphant
to the room   in sudden fear I know
no matter how I hide I cannot escape
I can never be rid of you

Infinity: Questions on a Troublesome Subject

Is everything that ever happened
locked in space
impressed on eternity?
are two young lovers caught there
saying goodbye over and over
singing the words to their song
"we may never meet again"
but not believing it
not able to believe
that as summer ends
their love will end
do they whisper
"are the stars out tonight"?
does the scent of honey-suckle
linger on the midnight air?
they are very young
and very sad
if they could stay forever
locked in each others arms
would they with foredoomed knowledge
choose   for that last desperate kiss
such a cycle of joy and pain
endlessly repeating itself?

Night Walk

A faint frost stars the earth tonight
and as I walk, beneath my feet
the hard ground glistens diamond-white,
the winter air is sharp and sweet.
Now I who burned with hot desire
yet lived to know how freezing feels,
who saw the past in frozen fire,
have learned at last the winter seals
that bind the land in silver shrouds,
a world of beauty numbed by ice,
will melt and pass in lifting clouds
as time and season break their vise.
The sun that is the core of day
to sleeping heart and earth will bring
in bud-thick branch, in fragrant spray,
another love, another Spring

I Have Come in to Quiet Waters

I have come into quiet waters
the raging sea subsides.
Far far ahead the future
like a boat in calmness rides.
My shallow craft is beaten,
Tiller nor sheet nor mast
will ever pull in wind again
for the fighting days are past.
Land-locked in the room of memory
I shall sit still and apart
though I hear the blast of thunder
shake roof and wall and heart.
But oh, will I ever remember
in some lost and dream-dim way
remember in gravest wonder,
how violent lightning shook me
how the lightning that was you
brightened and blinded me that day?

The Sad Dark (after Katherine Mansfield)

Ah, no! The sad dark does not lie within this night
though restless now I rise and leave the room I know.
Far from its friendly warmth and its protecting light
called by some ancient driving blackness I must go.
Unchanged the harbour lights, unchanged the night-birds cry
whose solitary sound captures my own despair,
the drift of summer smoke, one pine against the sky
and the west wind blowing, blowing on face and hair.
In this familiar darkness I have stood before
where green and terraced slopes lead to the cooling sand
where ghostly breakers glide and spill upon the shore,
and yet, tonight I cast no shadow where I stand.
Divorced by death from all the dearest I have known
the sad dark lies within the heart, bleak and alone.

What Wind Blows?

What wind blows
tearing days apart
sends time scurrying
bares the wounded heart?

What sense of sadness
falling softly here
brings lost summers
painfully near?

Bleak wind of knowledge
blowing down the day
echoes sadly, sadly
"all shall pass away."

I Have Been Betrayed

I have been betrayed
a fraction of my day
but how was this betrayal
I find it hard to say

I took my heart from beauty
to lay it on a thorn
and then cried out in wonder
to find it cruelly torn

The world of men beguiles us
it leads us with a smile
to dally on the wayside
to walk a crooked mile

A single kiss's tidal wave
can circle all the earth
The grave-deep knell of love
starts tolling at its birth

Had I but stayed with beauty
and given it my care
this too-impulsive heart of mine
might find the world still fair!

McMaster Farm Revisited

By the sagging doorway
in the bracken and tangle
of the weed-grown garden
where fruit and berries mingle
in the shade of the barren lilac
I stand   unable to recapture
even a sense of loss
rotted roof   sunken stairwell
grey timbers falling   this is
a deserted house on a wild hill
    nothing more
memory comes back
with faltering footsteps
for I can't regain and
the heart can't feel
what was once left behind
that joy of an earlier love
has been buried and mourned
and its ghost laid forever
I am a stranger here
there is nothing
except uneasiness
to haunt this hill
    and my heart

A Decent Burial

What shall we do for decent burial?
The mourners are suitably dressed
as they approach the grave
but their eyes ask questions
What requiem shall we sing
what necessary words say
over this cold clay and who
is the dead we solemnly await?
Only she   raw in grief knows
they are burying Tomorrow

Rejection

I must not think of him
from this day on,
now and forever
his memory must be gone.
No matter in what manner
the empty days pass,
as the slow fall of rain
on small spring grass,
as fine-feathered flakes
of muffling snow
covering the dark earth
that sleeps below,
he shall be shut from me
as though laid in the grave
and no one must know
the store of tears I save.
Now shall the thoughts
that I hold of him
lie far and forbidden
as the closed grave's rim

Love is a Growing Thing

Love is a growing thing
it must increase
or wither at the root
it must have petal fall
to bear its fruit
love turning inward
unable to expand
means barren harvest
and empty hand
with love the world
becomes our child
its first felt movement
sweet and wild
from such a seed
we shall begin
to circle eternity
and draw it in

The Promise

The house stands still unchanged
where windows look to the lake
and leaning there in the moonlight
last night I tried to take
a long trip backward in time
to hear the words you had said,
not knowing one can't rekindle
fire from the lips of the dead.
The angry sound of your voice
invaded the moon-drenched room
but its echo was lost in thunder,
drowned by the waves' deep boom.
I felt the world diminish
that night when you turned away,
but I vowed I wouldn't speak. . .
and I kept that vow till today.
Let me tell it, dear traitor,
secret too late to keep,
now, as then in the night-time,
I was betrayed by sleep,
for all night long
the strong wind blew
and all last night
I dreamed of you.

The World is Still

the world is still   so still
a bird's small single note
cuts through the mind
with painful sharpness
this is the time of emptiness
when the heart for a moment
rests in tranquility
still as the air   quiet as the land
this is no time to cultivate the past
dig from the memory tired hurt
and pain and old lost loves
those blighted roots   shadows now
receding on the fields of yesterday
this is no time
to dream of tomorrow
magnifying fears and sorrow
or to anticipate happiness
a thing as elusive as sunlight
on swift summer water
here   for a fractured second
rest still   do not dream
be one with the quiet day
with the single note
as it falls
away and away

III

Sonnets

I Had Forgotten You

I had forgotten you until today
When from another's lips I heard your name
Star-shaken memory bore the years away
And laughing from the dead young past you came.
Tonight the summer wind blows from the south
And I, a pilgrim, once again must search
For dreams that linger hotly on my mouth
Remembered kisses and the heart's faint lurch.
On every side the roses burst in flame,
their beauty like the world's first lovers, old.
Above us, one by one, star-blossoms came
A thousand shining in the sky's dark fold.
Forgotten perfume of a frail young rose,
It is a ghostly kiss the old wind blows.

I

From what wild hunger comes my need of you?
A small seed planted in the womb of Time
When Eve first took forbidden fruit and *knew,*
In that same hour began its upward climb.
What had before been innocent and clean
Now thrived in darkness and in sure decay.
It was like all things sweet and young and green
Doomed to be mortal and to waste away,
This was the burden to be borne by men
That Time should ever bring as sorrow's part
Down the sad years to love and lose again,
But O my Dear, deep-rooted in your heart
It was so written, as the stars must be,
I am the ripened fruit of you, the tree.

II

How shall I sing that once was blind and dumb
And spent my days in the unknowing dark?
I had no warning you would ever come
And with your presence stir the infant spark
That flamed my world to shining new delight.
I am most grateful to be born in you,
The radiant dawn that ushers out my night
And teaches me dead poets all sang true.
O do not leave me yet for I must know
The beauty that lies in me with you near.
You cannot give me life, then careless, go,
Returning me to darkness and to fear.
Rise up my songs on straight and swiftest wing
Although the lips are sealed, the heart may sing.

III

How like a dove my heart is borne to you
On swift straight wings and in unerring flight.
I hold this comfort to be deep and true
That it rests there by its own destin'd right.
No matter where we go, how far our ways,
You carry part of me so buried deep
That through the length and breadth of all our days
My wings shall beat upon you in soft sleep.
In waking you will always be aware
That no reluctant captive do I lie
It is by my desire I shelter there
And in your vital heart shall live and die.
An alchemy of fate brought you to me
Whose fledgling wings were aching to fly free.

IV

You play a clever game of cat-and-mouse
Now in full chase and now in full retreat.
I seek the safety of my prison-house
Who dare not go about in any street
Lest if you do not try to find me there
And solitude becomes a thing of pain,
heart-sick with loneliness I cannot bear,
I search to be rebuffed by you again.
Just now I bolted fast the heavy door,
Yet all the gathering darkness seems to fill
With waves of thought that wash the tired mind's shore,
Despair you will not come, despair you will.
With fearful joy, in the heart's wildest pause
Trembling, do I await the knife-sharp claws.

V

It comes again in darkest night to me
Who all unguarded in deep sleep lies twined,
The rising tempest and the swelling sea
Of fear that mount the ramparts of the mind
To storm the inner reaches of the heart.
When black the waves break on this secret shore
And I my habit-chains must wrench apart
To thrust myself against their hurl and roar,
Then let me stand in foam breast-deep
And shout defiance with my head held high.
I am no coward though assailed in sleep,
I know they fight who do not will to die.
Spent as the waves that creep across the sand,
War-weary now, I seek sleep's welcome hand.

Premonition

A golden moment held in time tonight
between faint sorrow and a sigh suspended,
this hour of sweet familiar things brings light
yet why have voices hush'd, the music ended?
I would hold fast the world now if I could,
unchanged each gesture and each person here,
a frieze of flesh not marble or carved wood
immobilized forever, warm and clear.
A darkling stranger hovers low to lay
its cold hand on the unsuspecting heart
so words half-spoken slowly drift away
and friends in sudden silence draw apart,
for into this young night unsought, despair,
as Autumn's chill comes creeping, fills the air.

For My Mother: A.G.D. 1962

I did not know he sat so close. It seems
if half-remembered childish fears are true
when trembling I awoke from feverish dreams
of dancing bones and called aloud for you,
there should have been some terror in this place,
a dark foreshadowing, and not the blaze
of joy and heightened beauty in your face
that made a rosary of those last days.
I asked, still glowing from your lovely light,
in brief bewilderment, why others wept
when this sweet presence overwhelmed the night,
for watching by your bed I thought you slept.
No, not till later did his icy breath
proclaim this gentle stranger to be Death.

About The Author

Leila Pepper has been writing prose and poetry for more than half a century. She is a Windsor writer who studied with W. O. Mitchell at the University of Windsor. She has written two other books for Black Moss Press — Caught In Amber, and In War With Time.